I Don't Care!

Written by Brian

Illustrated by Mike

sundance

A Haights Cross Communications ✕ Company

Kids Corner Books

KID-TO-KID BOOKS

I Feel Angry	I Feel Bored	I Feel Bullied	Excuse Me!
I Feel Happy	I Feel Jealous	I Feel Frightened	I Don't Care!
I Feel Lonely	I Feel Shy	I Feel Sad	I'll Do It!
It's Not Fair	I Feel Worried	Why Wash?	It Wasn't Me!

LITERACY STORIES

Dogs Can't Read
Mice Can't Write
Spiders Can't Spell
Cats Can't Count

All rights reserved.
This edition published
in North America by
Sundance Publishing
P.O. Box 1326
234 Taylor Street
Littleton, MA 01460

First published in 1997 by Wayland Publishers Limited
Copyright © 1997 Wayland Publishers Limited

ISBN 0-7608-3922-0

Printed in Canada

In the corner today,
we're talking about

being respectful.

This way to Kids Corner

3

Ever since I was little,
I've heard people talk about respect.
I didn't really know what they meant.

Oh, I know all about heroes.

It's easy to respect
famous people
who have done
great things.

But Grandpa says
that I can respect everyone I see.

I think he might be right.

I respect my mom.

I respect my teachers.

7

Sometimes I have to look hard
to find things to respect—
like when Roger
was really mad at us,
but he didn't take his ball
and go away.

8

But it gets easier
when you see how it feels
if someone doesn't respect you—
like when you make a mistake
and someone teases you.

I'm getting good at showing respect.

I try to remember
that not everyone
loves a parade
in the morning.

And when I see that people want quiet time, I take my parade somewhere else.

11

I never give secret haircuts—
even when I think
someone really needs one.

And I know that
paint works best
on paper.

I know that the park is for everyone.

Some people don't think
that Rufus is the best dog ever.
So we try to find other places to play.

NO DOGS
(OR CATS)

Sometimes
I forget that
some people
don't think
my Super Flip
is the best trick ever.
So I ride someplace else.

No Skateboarding

I respect others by keeping
public places neat and clean.

I never litter,
even if the trash can is full.

16

And I'd never paint on a wall or a statue.

Like I said, I only paint on paper.

When I'm camping, I try to remember that other campers don't want to hear me sing when they're asleep— no matter how good I am.

I respect other readers
by taking care of library books.

It's hard to read a book
that has jelly all over it!

NO EATING
IN THE LIBRARY!

I don't think I'd want
any of them
trying to catch <u>me</u>!

I can show respect
by being thoughtful and nice—
even if my dog is too sleepy to notice.

I know how good it feels
when other people are nice to me.

23

At a show,
I listen quietly
when people perform.
And I always clap
when they're done—

even if they squeak
once in a while!

24

I feel pretty bad when
people don't show me respect.

It feels really good when
other people let me know
that they care about me.

And that
makes me want
to do my best
for them.

When I respect other people
and they respect me,
I feel good about myself.

And then I respect everybody, especially myself.

Things to Do in the Kids Corner

Choose a person you respect. Write a letter to that person telling why you respect him or her. If you want, deliver or mail your letter to the person.

Write five questions about *I Don't Care!* Quiz a friend to see if he or she can answer your questions. Then see if you can answer your friend's five questions.

Pretend you are a spider. Write a poem telling people why it's important to respect you and not squish you. Draw a picture to go with your poem.